BALANCING ACT
Strategies for Successful Aging

BALANCING ACT
Strategies for Successful Aging

Sandra Conant Strachan

2017

Balancing Act: Strategies for Successful Aging
© 2017 by Sandra Conant Strachan

Identifier: ISBN 978-1-387-34084-2

All rights reserved. No part of this book may be reproduced in any form or by any means, electronic or mechanical, including photocopying, recording, or by any information storage and retrieval system, without permission in writing from the author.

First Edition
Printed in the United States of America

Designed and desktop publishied by David M. Dunn, Mirror Communication

All proceeds from the sale of this book will be donated to programs in Central America that provide education and health for children and adolescents.

To my parents, Frances Louise James Conant and Allah B. Conant, who taught me more than they know about life, love, and growing old.

CONTENTS

Preface ix
INTRODUCTION 1
CREATING POSITIVE NARRATIVES . . . 19
ATTITUDES THAT MAKE A DIFFERENCE . 33
COPING WITH VALLEYS 43
A PALETTE OF STRATEGIES
    FOR SUCCESSFUL AGING 57
    1. Strategies for building social networks. . 59
    2. Strategies for physical well-being . . . 63
    3. Strategies for mental growth. 74
    4. Strategies for economic well-being . . . 76
    5. Strategies for spiritual deepening . . . 84
    6. Strategies for creating your legacy . . . 91
WHEN IS IT TIME TO CREATE
    A NEW FUTURE? 99
FINAL THOUGHTS 113
EPILOGUE 125
Recommended Reading 128

PREFACE

I'll be 72 years old on my next birthday and I'm shocked.

It's hard to define the difference between the 35-year-old self that lives inside me and the woman who looks back from the mirror. Yes, I've had more experience. Yes, I've learned more about what I value and what I don't. Yes, some things that were simply "problems" when I was 35 are now "heart-breaking realities." Things that were heart-breaking have become pin pricks. Things that were once fulfilling have been replaced by new passions. Of course I'm different on the outside, but it seems I'm still having to learn some truths over and over again.

I have a cartoon on my desk. A gerbil sits pensive and bewildered in the door of his cage, while a second gerbil races frantically around his. The first gerbil is saying, "I've had an epiphany." I'm still waiting on mine.

I want enlightenment that helps me come to grips with aging and see the rich challenge of this phase and what follows. Having accompanied my mother to her one hundredth year and end of life, I have enormous sympathy for anyone who is both child and caregiver. It's a tightrope that is simultaneously awful and awe-full. As an older woman, I know how much daily struggle is unspoken by the elderly, and I hope to give voice and courage to many.

A perspective of Life as a learning lab is essential to our capacity to change and a great gift with the passing of years.

So I write for two main groups of people. First, I'm writing to those between 65 and 95, the ones most likely to have daily confrontations with redefining their lives and figuring out "what now?" in the face of new challenges. They experience how it feels to grow old rather than merely talking about it. Second, I hope to speak to people between 35 and 75 who have older parents and/or friends they're caring for. If the folks are aging well, this can be a halcyon time as mutual love and appreciation deepen. But if the parents or friends are trapped in denial, anger or inertia, it can be hell. I have been on both sides—as a daughter and as an elder—and I prefer the latter.

I believe strongly that we make our lives, which is *not* equivalent to controlling them. We have different childhoods, careers, strengths and weaknesses. Some of us grow old alone, others are surrounded by family and friends. We are dealt certain cards, but we see winners who win with the same hands that losers lose with. One person succeeds against a stacked deck while another fails even though he has every asset. *Why* is a mystery. That some people are resilient and creative and others not is baffling. The only common denominator is that in successful lives, *every experience* is viewed as an opportunity to learn. The worst things teach us and the best things teach us. A perspective of Life as a learning lab is essential to our capacity to change and a great gift with the passing of years.

Aging is just another room in the lab, set apart, yet connected to the whole building we call our lives. Everyone I talk with has a unique tale to tell. Every story has different characters, challenges, and outcomes; every person has unique potential. But that said, there are universal themes that run through the personal sagas and create a web of shared experience. My own life is simply one example, but I share my story to connect with you, raise questions that need answering, and offer ideas for opening up possibility.

Introduction

If you're reading this, you've probably had the *aha!* experience of getting old.

This awareness may occur at 40 when you suddenly can't read anything less than 20 inches from your face or when you play basketball and can't walk the next day. It may come at 50 when your marriage falls apart and you're back in the dating game. Maybe the moment waits until you're 60 and a parent dies or two of your high school friends get cancer. If you're 70 and it hasn't happened, it may be time to wake up to reality.

In spite of blips of awareness, most people ignore their aging until the symptoms become persistent. People like to say that age is just a number. I want to say, "Try telling your body that." Denial is an option, but it's far from a solution. Yes, you can deny the "small cuts" along the way that are reminders of where the path is going, but denial has no survival value, and its overuse becomes a major block to aging well. Why? Because aging is science, not magic. Getting old is not an illness to be cured. Parts wear out and slow down. The speed with which they do so may be due to genes, overuse, misuse, environment or simply the way it is, and all the denial in the world won't make it go away. Aging is unavoidable.

I can look at the future as a slow slide into decrepitude or I can use the period from 65 to 85 to get ready for what comes next. That's 20 years, folks.

Aging *well*, however, is an art, or more accurately, a learned skill.

After the age of thirty, it's hard to pretend that you're still a kid, even if you're still living

Introduction

at home and don't know what you want to do. At forty, your adulthood is undisputed, seen by many as the period of highest potential and energy. This decade is often an important time for building a reputation and career. Then come the fifties and the last decade you will rarely think about getting "old." After all, you still look good, you can do almost everything you want—travel, run, work long days. Major illnesses happen to other people, or so it seems.

Then a good friend has a heart attack. Your parents are showing their age and need more attention. If you have kids, they are finishing high school or college, beginning to imagine where they will work and live, and you are increasingly peripheral to their lives. From sixty on, we suffer increased physical changes like less stamina, occasional achy joints, and problems with vision, smell or hearing, but it's still manageable. Emotionally, you may reach the end of the rope in a bad marriage, or in a good marriage, discover a fresh desire to create memorable moments as a couple and family. You may find that your beloved job is somehow less interesting and satisfying. So maybe you retire or divorce or both, only to realize that the moorings of your life are gone. At first, this feels like freedom, and it is, but some freedom is onerous and some releasing.

Then one day you're 70, and a similar thing happens as happened at 30. Only you can't pretend that your life is half over. You won't live to be 140. So what now? This is a tough question because you may be looking at another 20–30 years on the planet. Whoa! That's practically a whole lifetime. Unfortunately, it's the last one.

Lawrence Frolik is a professor at the University of Pittsburgh School of Law and an expert on housing options for the aging. In a classic article describing the potential housing needs of the aging, Frolik says:

> Younger individuals often look upon retirement as a homogenous age period; that is, everyone over the age of sixty-five is about the same. This is inaccurate. Gerontologists like to classify old age into three periods: the period from age sixty-five to seventy-five sometimes called the "young old"; the period from age seventy-five to

Introduction

eighty-five sometimes called the "old"; and the period post age eighty-five, sometimes referred to as the "old old." The division of old age into three periods highlights the reality that old age can conceivably extend for thirty years, from age sixty-five to ninety-five. Over that potential thirty-year plus span, the wants and needs of the older individual will change. More specifically, their housing needs will change (Frolik, 1997).

The good news: There are phases. The bad news: Housing may be the least of your worries.

So according to Frolik's definition, I'm young-old—but "old" is still part of the equation. There are several different ways to approach this information. I can look at the future as a slow slide into decrepitude or I can use the period from 65 to 85 to get ready for what comes next. That's 20 years, folks—plenty of time to plan for decrepitude.

As I begin this, I am a few months past the death of my 99-year-old mother, Fran. Let me tell you a little about her: She was born, raised, and lived until she died in Waco, Texas. She was a product of the Depression, married at 21, two children (one born pre-WWII, the other post-war.) She was adored by her husband and spent her life as a homemaker, despite a desire to work in a *real job* (or so she said). She was tiny in stature, but tough-minded, disciplined, introverted, pragmatic, fair, and a good mother.

She aged beautifully, to all appearances rarely beset by thoughts of what might happen if Daddy pre-deceased her. He did so without warning on a December day in 1992 when they were in their mid-70s. Mother lived alone for the next 22 years, finally agreeing to move into a retirement home at 97 when she began to fall more frequently. The center was not assisted living, but rather a place where able-bodied and able-minded elders lived, many of them former teachers and most between 85 and 100 years of age.

Not quite a year into her new home, she developed pneumonia and almost died. She entered a local hospice program because doctors discovered pulmonary fibrosis, a terminal condition. After two weeks at death's door, she got fed up with dying, went into rehab and moved back to her center with great relief and

Introduction

fanfare. About 15 months later, after a period of dramatic weight loss and increased debility, but with little loss of mental capacity, she died quietly, appreciative of the love and care she received during her final two years.

As we age, we're captains of a ship on a very different sea than we've ever sailed before. Our destination is the final port of call.

For me, the whole process of watching her as an old, old woman was a revelation. I see much more in retrospect than I saw at the time—many more signs of decline, many more reasons for her choices, which often seemed stupid, capricious or delusional. I'm aware of more deception on her part. I only saw what she wanted me to see. I am amazed by her strange self-absorption. For instance, I tried to encourage her to move or stop driving by pointing out that my brother and I were worried about her. *Her* response was that she knew that. Her unspoken response was "and I don't care. Maybe it's time you worried about me for a change." What she wanted took on a new primacy as if she had been robbed of that for too many years.

With distance, I can think of ways I might have enabled her to acknowledge her limits with more clarity and acceptance. But maybe not. We each take this journey in our own way, and those closest to us are often the people we least heed. But I intend my journey of aging to be different, and I want yours, dear reader, to be different as well. We need to be more honest, creative, and proactive in our final years. After all, we are the only people who aren't mere bystanders in our aging and dying.

Let's wake up to the fact that we're going to get old. Every aspect of the way we have lived to now and how we need to live into the future will need re-examination. What was a valid response at 30 will probably not be valid at 80. Our personalities and self-perceptions may not change. If we're stubborn, we may die stubbornly. If we disdain any hint of dependency, such as accepting help or graciously receiving a gift, we may die fending off every offer of assistance that comes our way. But poor us. If we

INTRODUCTION

think for a minute others will find us "brave" or "independent," or "fun to be with", think again. If we continue to shield our kids (even the ones who are now 50 or 60) from the truth of our lives, we are doing them a disservice.

Staring The End *in the face with eyes wide open and simultaneously throwing ourselves into life with passion and optimism—this is* the *balancing act of all time.*

In other words, we must be more truthful, open and direct about what's happening—both with ourselves and others—and more conscious of how we manage growing old.

It is possible to age gracefully, but as the saying goes, it ain't for sissies. It's hard because you and I have to give up long-held traits and beliefs—the very notions that have given us the full life we wanted. As we age, we're captains of a ship on a very different sea than we've ever sailed before. Our destination is the final port of call. It is a new world. The pitfalls, possibilities, fears, and hopes are all different in this phase of life.

"Re-definition" is key in figuring out this unfamiliar landscape. Think for a moment about the notion of independence. Many people say the loss of independence is the most hateful thing about aging. "I *never* want to lose my independence. I can lose my vision or be unable to walk, but for God's sake, let me go before I become dependent." Okay, so you pride yourself on your independence. Society, your parents, boss, friends and relatives, all tout this as one of the highest-rated character traits in the world:

> *Don't depend on anyone, don't ask for help, don't let on that you're suffering, keep driving 'til they take your license away and live in the same home for 30 or 50 years even though it has three flights of stairs. Make your own decisions, call your own shots.*

These voices hound us. The truth is, however, that the longer we live, the more likely that a rigidly-defined sense of independence will become a semi-suicidal straitjacket. Imagine the moment when *they* do take away our license, we're stuck at home, we've never called a taxi, and we're not about to now. We're also not

Introduction

going to take one of those old-people buses that do home pick-ups. So if we have a kid living nearby, we guilt him/her into helping. We rationalize, "After all, we carted them around all those years." If there's no child or Good Samaritan available, we stay home a lot, and pray that maybe someone will come to visit. Some people starve to death doing this.

Here's an alternative scenario: You lose your license. You loathe the idea of being a burden to your kids. You loathe being dependent on anybody. But you're going to go crazy if you don't figure this out. So you re-define "independence" from "not needing any help" to "deciding the help I need and finding it." Then you explore ideas: call a taxi company to find out rates and if a regular driver can be assigned; locate the elder service programs in the area and find out their offerings; ask around to see if there are volunteers at the church or YMCA or community college for people who need help from time to time. Make a plan. You are in control. You are proud. You are making decisions. You are taking the reins of your life. And you are independent.

After a certain age, we walk a tightrope between two dramatic and apparently incompatible realities. On the one side, science says that the systems that control body and mind are in a decline that will eventually lead to death. (A detailed explanation of the physical aspects of aging can be found in Sherwin Nuland's *How We Die*.) On the other side, we still have energy, will, freedom, imagination, and time to explore life until death shows up. Staring *The End* in the face with eyes wide open and simultaneously throwing ourselves into life with passion and optimism—this is the balancing act of all time.

Yes, you're more vulnerable. For the first time, you may buy cancellation insurance for a vacation cruise or a trip to New York. But does that mean you don't take the trip? No way. Yes, stamina is limited and standing in long lines or climbing hills wears you out. Does this mean you don't fly to Arizona to see the Grand Canyon? No. You get a wheelchair in the airport, you stand on the rim, then watch a film about going down into the canyon on a mule. My Aussie friend Liza showed me a delightful way

Introduction

of coming to terms with limitations. When she was in her late 70s and had to use a wheelchair getting on and off airplanes, she said that rather than feeling humiliated or ashamed when people stared, "I simply imagine I'm the Queen."

We are all victims of what I call "age-related schizophrenia"—the experience of being a 35-year-old in a 75-year-old body.

There is a story attributed to the Cherokees about an old Indian instructing his grandson. The old man tells the boy, "You have two wolves fighting inside you—one who is angry, hurtful, vengeful, greedy, self-absorbed, and the other who is kind, loving, generous and giving. They fight constantly inside you and inside others as well." The boy asks, "But Grandfather, which wolf will win?" And he answers, "The one you feed."

All of us harbor the wolves of aging—-one who focuses on how bad things are, how much we have lost, the unfairness of debility, the sadness, the fear, and another who focuses on the freedom, the wisdom gained, the opportunities to give, the blessings received, the lessons learned. These wolves fight constantly and each one wins from time to time for they are evenly matched, and frankly, because we feed both of them. But aging well means steadily nourishing the second one in order to achieve an understanding that even the end of life is full of surprises, gifts and learning.

I recently had a conversation with my sister-in-law, Marie, a woman who has suffered many years with multiple sclerosis. I asked her advice on what she has learned about coping with a chronic illness that is characterized by pain, loss of coordination and memory, and constant unpredictability. I asked because she's been an excellent example of positive, loving, adventurous energy. And I asked because I am entering a phase that includes chronic attacks of aging, waking up some days too tired to move, others with unexpected pains and loss of balance, and more hesitation in the face of unfamiliar situations. I'm going blind, just as my mother did, and that's a downer. I rarely go to the doctor

Introduction

because I know he or she will smile, say that the blood test results are normal, comment that nothing appears to be amiss, and that the symptoms are probably "age-related." Then I have to decide if I believe this diagnosis. Sometimes you can't.

If this is the way it's going to be for the next thirty years, I want advice from a real expert, so I called Marie.

She had various suggestions, including being well-informed about her illness, finding a doctor she trusted, thinking prevention (like strengthening her hands before they get weak) rather than waiting for something to go wrong, meditating and praying. One of the first things she recommended was looking at the strategies that have worked in the past and applying them to current challenges. This means reflecting on the adaptive responses from your experience that can enable you during this time in your life. Be discriminating. If you were a compulsive workaholic, that might have made you a millionaire, but it won't make you a better old person.

My career was about helping people create strategies: I led workshops on both organizational and personal planning. I watched people discover new wisdom for themselves and for their businesses. Recalling the successful strategies in my life brings me to my objectives for writing what you're reading. I want to offer you:

- *Practical, easily integrated, daily strategies* for simultaneously balancing your acceptance of inevitable decline and exploiting the growth potential of aging
- *Actions* to help you live fully until your final breath
- *Ways to deal with the fearfulness* that comes with growing old
- *Options for acknowledging death* that go beyond obsessing about it or ignoring it

Each strategy offers a chance to wake up—not to the nightmare of decrepitude, but to the promise of life lived successfully, right to the end.

"Whole person/whole life" aging begins the moment you accept the fact that you're getting old and everything is in flux—your body,

Introduction

emotions, spirit, social relationships, mental maps and attitudes. We are all victims of what I call "age-related schizophrenia"—the experience of being a 35-year-old in a 75-year-old body. How do we recognize that and ensure a balanced realism? I want to share ideas that can help us age well. They are gleaned from people who have learned how. Along the way, I will mention wise authors with good advice. I hope to avoid fluff, get to the point, and make this a short read. I want to provide building blocks you can use to construct your life from here on. You're the architect, general contractor, and worker, all rolled into one.

CHAPTER 1

Creating Positive Narratives

In July 2016, I heard a talk by Bryan Stevenson, a lawyer who works with inmates on death row in Alabama. The topic of his presentation was race and justice. Afterwards, my husband Harry and I realized that there is a much broader application of one of his points—namely, the idea of *narrative*. Stevenson's emphasis was on our national story about race in America. He pointed out that there were many gaps—both in the history of race relations, the non-telling of things like lynchings or the lasting impact of Jim Crow laws, as well as in the present challenges we're facing. Stevenson has several great YouTube videos, a TED Talk, and a book,

Just Mercy, all thought-provoking and highly recommended.

As Harry and I discussed Stevenson's presentation, we became aware of our own narratives—stories about our lives, social issues, and other people. *Everyone* has many narratives. All of them directly and profoundly influence our *actions* and *behaviors*. Some are positive and life-giving, some are negative and stifling. Yet we seldom examine our narratives because in some way they work for us. Sadly, some are not healthy, and those are the ones that need re-framing.

Sometimes a story is life-enhancing, and sometimes it's so negative that we are blinded to the potential for growth and creativity.

I'm using the word *narrative* to communicate the same idea held in words like self-story, paradigm, personal myth, historical re-creation, or mental model. I like narrative because it suggests that these understandings are dynamic and can be changed. We write the novel of our lives, opinions, personas, and beliefs, not once, but over and over as we grow, learn, and age. A narrative is usually based on a collection of facts—verifiable realities unless you're delusional—but it takes those facts and interprets them in particular ways. An example is a woman I know whose mother was extremely active in civil rights in the 60s. My friend was always proud of her mother's courage and commitment. On the other hand, her brother deeply resented his mother because of a perception that he was neglected and that her children were always secondary to her cause. He blamed her for the anorexia that led to his death in his 50s. Same mom, same basic facts, very different interpretations and *very* different outcomes.

Our narratives about growing old, about dying and death, even about what comes after death, evolve over time. A twenty-year-old rarely thinks about any of these things, yet has an answer for each that fits his or her time in life. An eighty-year-old's narrative is based on experience and perspective. Sometimes our story is life-enhancing and sometimes it's so negative that we are blinded to our potential for growth and creativity. A faulty narrative can lead us to ignore aging as a factor to be reckoned with. We may know people who launch new businesses, organizations or building projects at an age when they should be winnowing. We have friends who do nothing with the last thirty years of their lives because they've decided they don't have the energy, creativity, or will to tackle something new.

The most important thing is the narrative they create for giving meaning to this change.

Is there a *right answer* or a *perfect narrative*? No, but there is a process that begins with a clear-eyed examination of one's situation (physical, mental, financial, emotional) and moves toward a positive, thoughtful plan to get you from where you are to somewhere you'd like to be. There is a realistic way to go forward. Each of us has many self-stories that hold our beliefs about our personalities, our pasts and futures, our successes and failures, our politics, community, and jobs.

Creating Positive Narratives

Life offers many chances, some not at all welcome, to re-think our narratives. A crisis is such a moment. It can be a simple crisis. For instance, I broke my foot and because of an infected dog bite on the same leg, I couldn't get a cast. This meant almost a month of bed rest with a raised leg before getting a boot. After initially cursing the injustice of it all, I realized it would offer rest, time for visits, guiltless reading, journal writing, phone conversations with far-away friends. I went from a "poor me, I'm gonna go nuts" narrative to a "wow—what a relief!" narrative. My foot stayed broken and I did have days of going a little crazy, but on the whole it was a positive experience. Obviously, for the crisis to be an opportunity rather than a disaster, we have to recognize our narratives and then seek one that helps us live in the reality.

There are also complex crises. I know a couple in their 40s. Both are successful and living the good life in a large city with their two young children. The husband, a doctor, was diagnosed with an illness that will end his career. Boom, just like that, the future morphs into something terrifying. So he and his wife are facing a terrible and frightening situation, but like others in dire moments, the narratives they choose will make all the difference. They can live out of tragedy or hope. They can live out of regrets over the past and what used to be or imagine a future with new possibilities. They can blame each other or support each other. They can change their priorities and routines or not. But one thing is for sure: No magic will change the facts.

The most important thing, therefore, is the narrative they create for giving meaning to this change. Because it is also a fact that there are new limits and new possibilities for a different future than they had planned.

Age has a way of speeding up these crisis moments. Situations that demand attention to narrative come with more ferocity than in the past. Change increases, loss increases, and unexpected issues increase, each of which is an opportunity to reinvent our stories. Negative, unempowering narratives that lead to anger, contempt, or despair *must* change if we want to live well. A crisis like going blind, breaking a hip, living in a too-big house, or getting fired provokes us to reinvent our lives. And this is when narratives take on new relevance.

Positive narratives connect us; negative ones separate us....The fact that you can change narratives is extremely empowering.

My husband had two insights I want to share. His first insight was that narratives are *selective*. Think of how you describe your childhood. You can summarize your first twenty years in 10–15 minutes. Why? Because you select the events that tell the story you want to tell. If it's a sad story, you choose sad events. If it's a happy story, you choose happy moments. We put things in and leave things out. Some we forget, others we willfully dismiss or ignore, and still other things simply never entered our consciousness. The truth is that almost anyone's first twenty years had some good and some bad, some love and some neglect, some support and some criticism—not in equal measure, but still there. Our history is a selected list of experiences that our minds filtered over time. We may not do this consciously, but we do it.

The second insight is that a narrative is *multi-layered*. If I say that my mother was "always" critical of me and that her reaction to any honor I won was "don't let it go to your head," I'm not lying. But I've made a selection of the things I choose to remember and that is only the first step in examining a narrative. I can also remember times when my mother sewed a special dress or said something nice. So other questions need answering: Why was *criticism* my interpretation of her reaction? Why was that all I heard? How did her attitude affect my life then and now? What have I learned? Telling only one version of my history is superficial and neglects many other layers that shape my beliefs, actions, and self-image. Understanding these layers of meaning can lead to new insights.

Positive narratives connect us, negative ones separate us. The best narratives awaken our ability to hear other perspectives. The worst narratives lead us to make others the enemy or define them as selfish or stupid. Positive narratives create positive results. Negative narratives leave us in a ditch of despair.

The fact that you can change narratives is extremely empowering. I don't have to live my life as the child of a critical mother. While I may stick with that story, I can change it to reflect that what I received as criticism may have been motivated by my mother's desire to be honest. Her harsh truthfulness has made me more aware of others' feelings and that sensitivity makes me more careful in my choice of words.

The knowledge that we can change is hugely important as we age. The old people we most admire are those who reinvent their narratives. They redefine their priorities and develop new understandings of what is important, who they are, and what the nature of their contribution is at different stages of life. The woman who was once beautiful, yet now accepts that she's wrinkled and hunched, is a person I admire. The man who ran a business empire and is now happy to raise a healthy garden shows an agility of spirit I hope to emulate. Their narratives have grown deep and green as the circumstances change. *That* is power.

The text box on page 29 has an exercise to start the process of becoming aware of your narratives. Re-examine any narrative that begins with the following phrases, and fill in the blanks. These questions will get you started, but keep asking. You will find that some of your narratives are healthy while others are designed to make you feel self-righteous and justified. Some are outdated; they worked when you were a kid, but now they don't. Some promote resentment or despair, and if perpetuated, will lead to a dead end.

Dare to ask yourself, "Do I know this is true?" Many self-stories are based on unspoken, often unflattering assumptions. My mom tended to assume the worst motivations in other people and was easily hurt. Perhaps this was behind her extreme introversion. When she moved to the senior residence, she struggled with that propensity. So-and-so said something ugly or was unkind. So-and-so ignored her. A woman who chewed her ice at every

> **REEXAMINING NARRATIVES**
>
> - *When I was growing up _____ .*
> - *I learned that to survive I had to _____ .*
> - *And I decided that when I was an adult I would _____ .*
> - *If only I had taken the path of _____ instead of _____ .*
> - *I'm really good at _____ .*
> - *I'm really bad at _____ .*
> - *If I just had _____ , life would be perfect.*
> - *I'm okay until you push this button— _____ —then I _____ .*
> - *I can't imagine living without _____ .*
> - *My life is unfulfilled because I haven't _____ .*

meal drove Mom crazy, and Mom assumed the woman *knew* that and did it on purpose. I learned later that another resident confronted the ice-cruncher about this habit and she was shocked that it was offensive to others. In my experience, very few people intend to hurt. Most are simply unaware.

Another friend told me, "My husband is robbing me of my real life." When I asked what her real life was, she said, "I don't know, but he's robbing me of it." Her narrative said that there was a "real life" she deserved, but couldn't have as long as she was married to this guy. The end result was that her disdain for him was palpable. She never examined her narrative, and it led eventually to divorce.

We all make negative assumptions, but it's important to question them. We impute meaning to the actions of spouses, friends, and acquaintances; we assume far more consciousness on their part than is actually there; we resent people we feel are violating our norms; and we assume that others are willfully wounding us when that never crossed their minds. I'm most often guilty of this with my husband. He does something, and I react negatively. If I don't examine this reaction, the end result is resentment. He and I have learned how better to test our perceptions and to bring them into the light of day, to discuss them to the point where we genuinely grasp the other's reasoning, even if we don't always agree. This process is key to all successful relationships, whether marriage, family or work. Assuming that most actions and reactions are not fully conscious can open a dialogue.

Consider this book an invitation to rethink and consciously retrofit your own understanding of the meaning of aging.

Psychiatrist Viktor Frankl wrote the book *Man's Search for Meaning* to chronicle his World War II experience in four concentration camps, including Auschwitz. He lost his parents, a sibling, and a pregnant wife, and endured the horrific day-to-day suffering of a prison camp. Even in these circumstances, Frankl observed, in others and in himself, that it was possible for an ordinary human being, even in an unbearable situation, to give meaning to life, to endure, and to retain hope in the future.

In the 27 years Nelson Mandela was imprisoned on Robben Island, he showed kindness to guards, one of whom said Mandela was a father figure to him. His subsequent release and career were remarkable for the absence of resentment or vengefulness.

As far as I know, neither Frankl nor Mandela used the word *narrative*, but both men's lives convey the extraordinary power of a positive, forgiving, meaning-filled story. You and I will probably never face such daunting circumstances, but we have the same opportunity to reinvent our narratives.

The notion of narratives infuses everything you'll read from now on. Consider this book an invitation to rethink and consciously *retrofit* your own understanding of the meaning of aging.

CHAPTER 2

Attitudes That Make a Difference

In addition to positive narratives, we have to develop positive attitudes. Things will happen over which we have no control, and the best laid plans for aging well may be sabotaged by Alzheimer's or other forms of dementia, brain injury, stroke, accident, or illness. So if your great plans for healthy aging go up in flames, does that mean you shouldn't create them? I say no. Go ahead, grab the possibilities, and work like crazy to live the way you want to live. Then if the worst happens and you lose control at the end, at least your last words won't be "Damn, why didn't I...?" As a side benefit, your friends and family will be amazed at your spunk.

Balancing Act

Positive attitudes are the bedrock of successful aging. But first we must come to terms with three hard, cold facts:

1. Aging involves loss.
2. The end result of every life is death.
3. 1 and 2 are true whether you have a good attitude or not.

In the arc of life, an end stage is inevitable. It may be early or late, sudden or gradual, painless or painful, normal or abnormal, but inevitably, there will be difficult changes long before the systems shut down and you stop breathing. I can hear you saying: "Haven't you heard of people doing Iron Man marathons at 85?" Yes, and there are also people who drop dead of a heart attack at 35. The statistics don't indicate that either of those scenarios is likely. Get a grip.

Physical changes show up in diminished energy, creaky knees, poor vision, and tiredness; more flu, colds, and "feeling bad"; and lessening of taste and smell, to name a few. Socially, you'll lose friends to death, dementia or orneriness. Psychologically, you may be more susceptible to depression. You may find it harder to feel passionate about anything or wonder why your once-fulfilling work seems humdrum. Mentally, remembering appointments or names is a challenge.

The bad news is that a good attitude won't make any difference in the reality of these losses. The good news is that certain carefully cultivated attitudes *make all the difference* in how you accept, appreciate, and respond positively to changes versus reacting with anxiety and denial. Consciously nurturing a positive outlook and certain "mental models" will have a huge effect on your relationships, your life style, and your sense of well-being.

Consciously nurturing a positive outlook and certain mental models *will have a huge effect on your relationships, your life style, and your sense of well-being.*

I'm using the word "cultivating" to suggest active processes like preparation, planting, and nurturing. Cultivating a plant is an active response within scientific limits. A tree starts with a seedling, and when it's watered, fertilized, and nourished with TLC, it flourishes and bears fruit. It's the same with attitudes.

In his book *The Tipping Point,* Malcolm Gladwell suggests that mastery of pretty much anything requires 10,000 hours of practice. If you want to age well, you have to practice at least that long. So you'd better get started.

We all know people who age admirably. Like that little old lady who danced with Michelle and Barack Obama at the White House. When asked what the secret was to dancing at age 106, she answered, "Just keep movin." My friend Suzanne tells of her grandmother, who, after receiving a terminal diagnosis, got the family together for one last home-cooked meal of their favorite foods. Everybody enjoyed the feast, said their good-byes, left for their homes and two weeks later, she died. Many of the over-90 folks in my Mom's retirement center are lively, alert, open, and full of laughter. I like being with them. I've discovered that if you want to feel young, don't hang out with youngsters. Hang out with the really old people who think that at 70, you're still a kid!

We also know people who demonstrate how we *don't* want to age. All they talk about is their latest illness, a veritable "organ recital" of all that's going wrong. They share the direst clips from the morning news, the most recent death of a friend, or yesterday's doctor visit. Their contributions to conversation run the same time-worn tracks to the same destinations, often atrophied even further by "my-way-or-the-highway" belief systems. They may be stuck in regrets and bitterness over unfulfilled dreams. They may be second-guessing decisions they made, like who they married or what jobs they took. Ugh. My point is: *attitudes make a difference.*

What are the key attitudes to cultivate?

1. *I am grateful.* Gratitude is perhaps the most fundamental building block of aging well, and it may be one of the hardest to cultivate. We measure whether a life has been "good" or "bad," a "success" or a "failure," using many yardsticks. Each person brings his or her own perspective and degrees of satisfaction or dissatisfaction. Our rating systems include categories like the abundance or lack of love and friendship, the

amount of money made, the level of recognition received for one's achievements, the depth of spiritual and personal growth, and the success of our children. Often life doesn't measure up to what we anticipated or hoped for, but a time comes when the only attitude that will take us forward is simply "I'm grateful for the life I've had." It's not that there aren't things you *want* to change. It's acknowledging that nothing in the past *can* be changed. It is what it is. You have learned, you have grown, and as Willie Nelson sings, "I woke up still not dead again today."

2. *I will approach every experience as an opportunity for growth.* When challenges come—including the big ones—don't run away. The loss of a spouse, moving to a retirement home, no longer being able to drive, are just a few of the events that can sink us, but it's possible to move on. Walk into the experience, invite the wisdom of others who have faced the same moments, be kind and patient with yourself as you chart a new course, look for the alternatives that free you to go forward rather than miring you in bitterness. It's possible to develop empathy, understanding, and wisdom from our struggles. I love the anonymous quote, "When something

bad happens we have three choices. We can let it define us, we can let it destroy us, or we can let it strengthen us." What isn't said is "We can let it teach us."

3. *I will be courageous and creative in the face of challenges.* Many folks believe that courage and creativity are in short supply, but that's a myth. It takes courage to call a cab or 911, try something new, buy an iPhone, take a cruise, try a new dish, or change homes. It takes creativity to break the bondage of "I've never done that before and I won't start now." Aw, go ahead. There's no better time to start. Take up painting or coloring books. Visit a chair yoga class. Write stories from your past. Take an online class. Ask a new person to sit at your table. The options are endless.

4. *I will focus on what I do have, not what I don't have.* No one escapes the loss and decline of aging. However, I'm younger today than I'll ever be again. The abilities I had at 30 are gone and the abilities I have today will be gone if I live long enough. It takes a lot of energy to bemoan these losses—so don't. Look at what you can do and give thanks. Then use your abilities for the well-being of others.

5. *I will be a blessing.* I will affirm, praise, encourage, listen, tolerate, empathize, sympathize, evoke laughter, build up, and engage everyone I meet. Furthermore, I'll let others do the same for me, and I'll say thanks and receive it graciously. This includes my family and friends, perfect strangers who offer their arms, the caregiver who gets me in and out of the shower, and the person who serves my food.

6. *I will laugh as much as possible.* Smiling uses fewer muscles than frowning does. Science has shown that laughter does more than just feel better; it actually changes your brain. This raises a chicken and egg question: Does humor help us find perspective or does perspective help us find humor? It's a conundrum I can't answer, but either way, humor and perspective are cousins, and finding the lighter side of your challenges awakens a new awareness of connection to other human beings facing the same or worse moments.

7. *As my outer world gets smaller, I will expand my inner world.* This is a tough one, but super important. As we age, many aspects of daily life become difficult or unwelcome. We have a tendency, well-documented in various studies, to withdraw and shrink our worlds to what we can manage with the

least difficulty. This is to be expected and accepted. After all, friends die and our social network gets smaller. Our vision wanes and we want familiar surroundings. It is harder to try new things, to read or watch the news, or even play cards. We don't have energy for the unfamiliar. But there are ways to keep our lives dynamic: listen to books and music, talk to friends, go for a walk, even if it's just down the hall, meditate, keep doing whatever you can do, and try one new thing a day.

These attitudes will take you a long way toward being the person you most want to be, even at this difficult stage of life.

CHAPTER 3

Coping With Valleys

I mentioned earlier that for many people, one plague of old age is depression. This is well-documented and the answer to "Why?" is pretty obvious.

First, age produces physiological changes in both brain and body. A chronic illness or history of depression in your family may be contributing factors, but even people who have never suffered a *clinical depression* may find themselves in one as they age. Key indicators for determining if ordinary sadness has morphed into clinical depression involve time, intensity, and frequency. *Has depression been a recurring pattern in your life? How long has a feeling of extreme sadness, fatigue, hopelessness or suicidal thoughts gone on?* If it's been several months, it's time to explore whether the condition has a physiological basis and can be helped with counseling or medication. One rule of thumb (a variable in the medical community) is that a depression that lasts longer than six months should be investigated. Don't be ashamed or wonder if you're "weak"—go to a good doctor. Be honest about the symptoms, and he or she will talk with you, ask questions, run a few tests and help you figure out next steps.

That said, even if the depression is unusual, but it improves with a few proactive strategies, it may be more "the blues" than clinical depression. Your sadness may be due to objective circumstances—a move, a divorce, a death. As noted, you're losing a *lot* of stuff. Capacities are disappearing, life is simultaneously a bullet-train and a tightrope, friends are dying and some of your fondest hopes are dying as well, looking in the mirror is a downer, your toes are miles away, etc. Geez, no wonder you're sad.

Coping With Valleys

According to the 1944 Harold Arlen-Johnny Mercer song, it's important to "Ac-Cent-Tchu-Ate the Positive," but unlike the lyric, it's a mistake to "eliminate the negative." Life is full of apparent opposites, but these polarities offer opportunities to more consciously balance the light moments with the dark ones, the plusses with the minuses. Integrating life's ups and downs is a matter of balance, but maintaining this balance is hard.

> *Suffering is too often bound up with wishing for a past that's gone or a future still hoped for and cursing the wretched present.*

My husband uses an analogy to illustrate the subtlety of integrating the ups and downs. We need certain nutrients in our diets. When a nutrient is lacking, the body reacts and gets out of balance. When we discover this deficiency, we decide how to adjust our diet to restore our health. I know, we can choose the food we eat, but we can seldom choose the events that impact us. No one asks for a broken hip or a lost job, but would we live as deeply if we never had to face challenges, if there were no tests to our resolve and imagination? Is there a certain amount of grieving, sorrow, suffering we actually need in order to maintain an equilibrium? Is suffering a nutrient? I don't know. But if our lives are best lived as a tapestry that includes darkness and light, joy and sadness, ecstasy and despair, it's worth considering that what we call "bad" might better be called "necessary." We are seeking a whole piece. Perhaps we should not think of life as "good" and "bad" but simply as "what is", and to constantly practice letting go of dichotomies that trap us into *either/or* thinking and take us away from integration and harmony.

The idea of depression (whether clinical or a bad bout of the blues) comes as a surprise to many of us. I consider myself to be a happy, steady person. I've never been susceptible to great ups and downs. I grew up with parents who had no tolerance for whining or self-pity. When a doctor asked my then 97-year-old mother if she ever felt depressed, Mom snorted and said, "Of course I do!" The doctor asked what she did when she was depressed, and Mother said, "I give myself a good talking to and say 'Get over it.'" I never heard my mother use the word "suffering" and in truth, I didn't use it until I was 69. I bought into the *give-yourself-a-lecture-and-get-on-with-it* mindset, and frankly, this approach has served me well for many years.

Then about eighteen months ago, a series of events catapulted me into a period of what can be reasonably called "suffering"—at least from my perspective. (A quick digression here: Suffering is relative. Being a victim of war, rape, hunger, poverty, abuse, mental illness, unrelenting fear—represents a level of suffering that I haven't experienced, and witnessing it leaves me speechless. So I don't use the word lightly, but I do use it to mean a state in which one's level of pain, anguish, sorrow, despair and loss is so intense that it's hard to see when it will end or to fully believe it ever will. Your head may know these things pass away, but nothing else in your being can see it. And most of us feel this way at least once, in spite of our minds telling us that others are much worse off than we are.)

My "dark night" included the terminal illness of my mother, a cancer diagnosis for my beloved brother, a seemingly irreconcilable conflict with my daughter and a 7-month bout of illness. As I write this, I can't honestly say it's over, though I believe I'm closer to accepting "what is." This type of suffering is too often bound up with wishing for a past that's gone or a future still hoped for and cursing the wretched present.

Being able to laugh and reaching out to others can expand our perspectives on the raw reality of what is happening.

This experience came in waves and layers. I spent a lot of energy giving myself pep talks and pushing myself out the door. When people asked how I was doing after Mother's death, I usually said, "I'm sad, but everything is fine." This wasn't a lie. I had time to reflect and write and share my emotions in the weeks after her passing. I had no regrets. For the most part I was the person I wanted to be in the weeks up to and after her death. I wasn't lying, but neither was I telling the whole truth; I was unconscious of the larger psychological-emotional-spiritual reality called "grief."

Then one evening, five months after Mom's departure, I was suddenly overwhelmed with sadness. The dark descended so quickly I was unaware how complete it was until my husband asked if I was okay. Here's the journal entry from the next morning:

> *I got in touch with a great sadness last night, just as I was going to bed. Part of the reason I knew that it was great was because even Harry could feel it radiating from me, as if he were more attuned to it than I was. And once I started trying to explain, I couldn't stop crying in a desperate attempt to make sense of it. I realized that I run from this, less because I'm afraid to face it, than because it feels so ungrateful. I don't have a right to feel this sad and dark given the glorious and bountiful blessings I enjoy—the love of and for a wonderful man, plenty of money, plenty of friends and dear ones, plenty of time to do as I please, trips and visits with interesting people, new adventures, swimming, art, on and on.*
>
> *But there it is. A shadow that invades and sits somewhere deep down and mourns. I mourn*

Mother, and our journey together, that there's so much I didn't understand or know or act on. I mourn my relationship to my daughter. I mourn my brother. I mourn my eyes and what losing them means as the world grows dim and I become more cautious & feel more vulnerable. I mourn my wrinkles and brown spots and striated drooping neck and fat belly and unexplained aches and pains and constipation and teeth that need fixing and being tired, tired, tired all the livelong day. All these things make me sad. They remind me of an end that may come long after I want it to or come too soon—either way to snatch me from this sweet old world. God, I enjoy this life. I love all those blessings. I love the challenges and I suppose at the bottom, I even love the mourning, just knowing that it's part of this life.

I think I need the tears to come, and perhaps they will. Maybe I'll find the time and place to wail my grief without the worry that it will cause Harry or anyone else pain to hear such sorrow. Alone enough to not feel embarrassed at such ingratitude. These sadnesses will not go away. They are as much my companions as God is, so thank God for God. They are the storms in a sunny life, and are perhaps even nourishing, though it's hard for me to see at the moment, flailing as I am in a flash flood.

Coping With Valleys

I remember lying in the sun one day and watching the clouds. They were heavy, and as they passed over the sun, it was obliterated for a time. The wind rose and the temperature dropped. And I was reminded that as gone as the sun might seem, it's still there. Even in the darkest night, it's shining somewhere and in the great cycle of being, it will reappear.

Joy will reappear. Gladness of heart will reappear. Deep gratitude will reappear. This isn't faith—it's fact.

Two days after writing this reflection, I read the following quotation from a blog I follow:

> Darkness is a natural part of life but I have fought this reality for years. Darkness always seemed like a powerful intruder into my light-filled life. I had this notion that if I thought or did the right things, then my life would always be full of light. I wouldn't have anguishing, dark times. Consequently, when the dark moments did come, I felt that something had gone terribly wrong with me. I presumed that I had failed in some significant way because I had not figured out how to keep the darkness out of my life. It has taken me a long time to recognize that darkness is an essential element (Joyce Rupp 1984, *Little Pieces of Light*).

Reading that blog was like the universe yelling in my ear. "*Hellllooooooo! You're not alone!*"

Knowing that others experience your pain reminds you that you're part of the human race. Yes, you're still alone because it's *your* pain and no one else's. All the self-talk in the world can't change or even assuage it much until some moment of insight hits you out of the blue.

The important thing to remember in these dark times is that you have to let yourself genuinely experience desolation while simultaneously cultivating attitudes and actions that give you hope. Humor and altruism are seen as the most effective coping mechanisms when disaster strikes. Being able to laugh and reaching out to others can expand our perspectives on the raw reality of what is happening.

So why am I sharing this? Because along with increased physical vulnerability in aging, we are also in danger of a psychological vulnerability that may catch us unaware. Like me, you may have spent most of your life "being strong," pretending to an invulnerability that wasn't always authentic. But old age is fraught with new challenges to your inner strength:

- Every death of a parent, a friend, a sibling, a spouse is a very particular loss because each relationship is unique and contains so much shared history. The loss of a friendship as the result of terrible misunderstanding is almost as great a loss as death. The resulting vacuum won't go away, even with the healing of time. These relationships won't be replaced. How can we *not* be saddened by that knowledge?

- It takes a lot of energy to develop and sustain a *persona*, that is the self the world sees—your personality. Doing so is part and parcel of being young, and so for the early and middle years, we don't mind the energy drain. However, as we age, we have less energy to devote to keeping up a front, regardless of how healthy and positive it may be. Worse, if we repress a lot of negative energy—regret, resentment, hurt, hate, shame—the energy needed to tamp it down is huge. Simply put, you get old and you run out of sufficient spunk to continue keeping up appearances. Slipping into the "Slough of Despond"* happens more easily.

---

* A deep bog in John Bunyan's allegory *The Pilgrim's Progress*.

- Many of things you worry about when you're 30 or 40 are mirages of a sort. They might happen, but there's a good chance it's your imagination working overtime. At 70 or 75, the things you're worried about tend to be more concrete and within the realm of possibility, even probability. You worry about going blind, being unable to walk, losing your spouse, or being alone and bankrupt at the end. These are real fears and without some initiative, they may be a part of your future.

Being sad is an authentic response. We shouldn't run from it or immediately attempt to defuse the feeling. It's a wake-up call: to consciousness, to making choices instead of being a victim, and to proactive efforts to manage even situations that are not "solvable." We should be caring enough to allow ourselves to feel bereft and to be patient with others when they're feeling likewise.

One of the saddest commentaries I ever heard was from a woman who had lost her husband in a plane crash. She was told by her mother-in-law, who was also widowed: "The world will give you six months to grieve. Then they'll wonder why you aren't over it." We must learn to give ourselves and others time and space to grieve.

If the valley is where you show up, then it is "what is." *Be there.* Travel its back roads. Look for its significance. Relax and know that the journey involves emerging and moving forward, that the sun is shining somewhere beyond the darkness. I have a friend who calls the pupa stage in a caterpillar's metamorphosis into a butterfly "life in the mush." The valleys feel like mush.

But valleys are part of an inner landscape that you now have time to explore. It's the landscape of meaning, of learning from each experience, of knowing yourself better. And aging opens the door to this in a way that is unique and positive. It's like the secret wardrobe or the hidden room that invades our dreams from time to time—a place of challenge and discovery.

CHAPTER 4

A Palette of Strategies for Successful Aging

This chapter offers a palette of practical strategies for successful aging. This is by no means an exhaustive set of options, but my hope is that the strategies that have served me well will spark your own imagination. One implication for your own strategic planning is to build, as my sister-in-law Marie puts it, a "personal lattice"— an underlying structure for your life. A lattice is "an interlaced structure, usually to support climbing plants....a trellis, grille, or grid." In this context, your personal lattice is the inner support system on which you hang activities. It helps you pay attention to your real priorities.

Balancing Act

One element of an effective personal lattice is a commitment of time to exercise. This time needs to include research into exercises that prolong abilities that may be in decline. For instance, Marie knew that both age and MS would lead to weakened hands. So she began hand-strengthening exercises, doing them as part of her morning routine and while watching television. Esophageal muscles may lose elasticity and cause difficulties in swallowing. A speech therapist can give you exercises to do when you brush your teeth or take a shower. Other elements of a lattice include setting aside time for solitude, reflection, or prayer, making sure you spend time with friends, and so on. In other words, designing a life lattice is a way of choosing and setting priorities that help you create the balance you want.

The following pages offer a variety of strategies in different areas. Use the check boxes to mark whether you are already doing it and a different mark to highlight if it's something you want to try. Leaving it blank indicates an inability or lack of interest in pursuing it.

1. Strategies for building social networks

As we age, our social networks become more vulnerable. We lose close friends with increasing rapidity. We may become less able to do regular activities and less interested in going out to lunch or traveling across the country to visit our siblings. Friends may be harder to be with if they sink into negativity or complaints. We have less energy and our enthusiasm for trying new things is declining. Ventures that used to give us pleasure, like regular cook-outs, an annual vacation, and Friday night soirées, begin to seem dull, drab, and routine.

Without our being aware of it, making the extra effort to change becomes more onerous. We give in to passivity and don't push ourselves to re-invent. We don't want to re-think our daily schedules, change homes, or go to unfamiliar places. Then one day, it dawns on us that "Honey, we've shrunk our lives."

Some react to aging by making life more manageable. They reduce their obligations or activities to suit their levels of stamina and enjoyment.

The opposite reaction is to get over-busy. We feel life slipping away and become anxious. The walls seem to be closing in, so we either avoid letting go of anything or add more and more activities. We fill up every waking hour with travel, clubs, and volunteerism, often in an unthinking way that eventually leads to feeling both physically and emotionally depleted.

Is there a third alternative? Here are some ideas:

- ☐ *Do a personal workshop.* In one column, put the activities you love and want to continue. In another column, write the activities that feel worn out and no longer fun. List any new explorations that interest you, like an online course, an art class, or a book you want to read. Lay out a typical week's activities and play around with revisions that provide options: more alone time or less alone time, more creativity or more rest, or just more of whatever you want now. Think about your body rhythm and chart your energy levels through the day. Think about your reflection rhythm: Do you keep a journal, daily, weekly, or monthly? If not, is that something you might try? Analyze what constitutes a balanced life—the mix of social time, solitude, entertainment, obligations, travel, staying at home, etc. Weight these elements to create a sense of equilibrium. Push yourself to design the life you want.

☐ *Engage in 1–3 new activities that expand your world*, get you into a new space and a new group of people, e.g., audit a class at the local community college, volunteer two hours a week at the hospital, be a greeter at Walmart—whatever. Don't fill up your life, but do something different.

☐ *Invite a friend you trust to help you do this thinking.* Ask each other questions.

☐ *Make the effort to keep in touch with people* via email, FaceTime, Skype, or actually writing a letter. (Whoa! a lost art!) You may not have the energy or money to travel, but you can still correspond enough to keep updated on the lives of friends and family. If you like to travel, arrange short weekend trips that are easily accessible for all parties. A friend of mine has a Third-Friday-of-the-Month lunch for five friends at a local restaurant. Anyone comes who can. No pressure.

☐ *Create opportunities for being with friends or like-minded people.* Music or art, a symphony or exhibition can become an occasion for getting together, for stimulating conversation and sharing thoughts. And there's always eating. A friend is in a club called "The R.O.M.E.O.s" (Retired Old Men Eating Out) that meets once a month to try a new restaurant. Another friend takes each of his grandchildren individually to lunch once a month. (He only has three.)

☐ *Investigate the over-50 community options near where you live.* These come in many shapes and sizes. Some are retirement centers, like my mother's, that have a monthly rental for a small apartment with meals, transport, and activities. Some are assisted living facilities that provide additional professional help as needed. There are CCRCs (Continuing Care Retirement Centers) that include an up-front payment and a comprehensive monthly fee for staged care from independent living, to assisted living or rehab, to full-time care facilities. The quality varies as much as the prices, so it's like visiting college campuses—you need to see them first-hand before making a decision. Do online searches or talk with friends and family to narrow the options. Visiting a place does not imply a commitment. Take someone with you and have lunch. The biggest advantage of a move like this is that it ensures a more immediate and caring community. If you worry about "being with all those old people," it's an unfounded fear. There are many opportunities for having friends from every decade—you just need to explore them.

Experimenting with activities like these puts us in charge of our social lives. Recognizing our own responsibility for our well-being is critical at every stage of life, but never more so than when we're aging. Our families are rarely the same as our friends and we shouldn't burden them with either being or planning our social life.

2. Strategies for physical well-being

Everybody and every BODY ages differently. Genes play a big part. I'm built just like my aunt when she was my age—thick in the middle and slope-shouldered. My sister-in-law Cathy can probably still fit into her high school graduation dress. On the whole, I have been very healthy, but I have friends, both older and younger, who have faced huge health challenges like cancer, MS, or diabetes. I am wrinkled from being a sun worshiper, but I have friends whose skin is still flawless. How you look and feel has a lot to do with relatives you never knew.

I maintain a good exercise routine and a healthy diet. Neither has helped me lose weight, reshaped my breasts, or shrunk my hips. Why do I keep it up? Here are my goals:

- *I don't want my last words to be,* "I should have exercised more and eaten less."
- *I want to feel better.* There's proof that exercise boosts endorphins and is good for your mind as well as your body.
- *I want to be proud of myself* and not feel like a slug.
- *I want to put my energy toward prevention* rather than cure.

Exercise won't eliminate ultimate decline, but I'm hoping it slows it down enough to make old age more pleasant. Here are a few ideas on exercise:

- ☐ *First and foremost, find something you enjoy doing.* For me it was discovering that I loved swimming. I never swam as a kid because it washed off my make-up and left me looking like a cross between a raccoon and a drowned rat. Then my husband invited me to do laps. I quickly discovered that I was lousy at coordinating breath and strokes, and I thought, "This wouldn't be a problem with a snorkel."

The first time I wore my snorkel to the country club pool, a guy snickered and said, "Not many fish down there, huh?" I transcended shame and still swim a mile 2–5 times a week.

The second hurdle was keeping count of the laps, so instead of counting, I have six sets of ten laps each, measured not in numbers, but in meditative themes. When I don't swim, I have a routine that begins with twenty minutes on the elliptical machine, twenty minutes of yoga, ten minutes of weights, and some dancing thrown in for good measure. My song of choice is Carole King's "I Feel the Earth Move"—I dance like a crazy woman, something I could never do in public.

For some people it's running, for some walking alone or with a friend, for others working in the garden or the kitchen, for yet others parking as far away as possible from the grocery store. Find what suits your personality and your body, then make time to do it.

☐ *Analyze your body rhythm and try to follow it.* I'm an early morning, straight-out-of-bed exerciser. If I miss that window, there's a 70% chance I won't do anything the rest of the day. (My bad.) Remember, there's enough time to do anything you decide to do. Aim for thirty to ninety minutes a day of intentional movement, not only formal exercise, but informal efforts to get your body in motion.

☐ *Buy a Misfit, FitBit, or Polar,* whatever device you like to help you measure your steps, your sleep, your pulse, and anything else you want to measure. Just having that on your wrist sets up a private contest with yourself. If you're highly competitive, you can share it online.

☐ *Decide if you're a groupie or not.* Some people flourish in a routine of classes. They like the camaraderie or accountability or fun of watching other people. Some are solitary—exercise is their thing done their way. I'm the latter. Group exercise makes me unhealthily competitive. Know thyself.

☐ *Vary the routine, but not enough to abandon it completely.* Give yourself a day off now and then, do your exercise at a different time of day, but never miss two days in a row if you can help it. The speed at which our brains "forget" how to move accelerates with age. The process is called "neuro-muscular amnesia." If you don't use it, you actually lose it and your brain has to retrain and reintegrate movement.

☐ *Follow the* three Ps *of exercise*: progressive, prolonged and programmed. "Progressive" means gradually upping the time or intensity of your exercise or consciously working different parts of the body. Age makes us less strong and energetic, so be careful to tackle a reasonable amount of more intense activity. "Prolonged" means committing for the long haul. "Programmed" means regularizing your exercise and paying attention to the whole body—flexibility, strength, balance and heart health.

There are also changes in how your body metabolizes food. It generally slows down and common wisdom is that you need to eat less. Here are some tips for a healthy diet:

☐ *Think small*. Small plates, small portions, small variety. Your aging body is less efficient at processing food, one reason many people gain weight. If you're blessed with a hummingbird's metabolism, eat all you want. But for the rest of us, it's important to recognize that we are probably satisfied with less food than in the past. If you go out to eat, share a main dish with another person. Skip dessert or buy one and share it with everyone at the table. Halve everything you eat and take the remainder home in a doggie bag.

☐ *Think nutritional value.* It doesn't take a genius to know that 200 calories of broccoli is better for you than 200 calories of tortilla chips. Most snacks are empty calories. Avoid them.

☐ *Read and listen.* You'd have to live on Mars not to know that the universal dietary recommendation is to eat lots of fruits and vegetables, less meat of any kind and as few sweets and breads as you can manage given that life is short. This is not rocket science.

Maintaining healthy exercise and diet routines *requires self-discipline and self-knowledge.* Chip and Dan Heath, the authors of *Switch: How to Change Things when Change is Hard*, characterize our inner battles with self-discipline as being like a rider on an elephant. The rider is our logical, rational mind; the elephant is our wild and crazy, emotional mind. If the elephant sees a danger or something it really wants, it will take off. Once that happens, the rider usually loses control. We all know the feeling.

Recognizing our own responsibility for our well-being is critical at every stage of life, but never more so than when we're aging.

There's no sure way to keep the elephant in check. When she wants to sleep in, eat two banana splits, or fall off the wagon, it will take a strong, canny rider to move her in another direction. A combination of personal mantras, a clear vision with feasible goals, and some social support helps me stay on track. Develop a few gimmicks as well. I had a diet plan that I called my "5S diet": no Sugar, low Salt, cut Starches, eat Small, no Spirits. The mantra was "Sugar! Salt! Starches! Small! Spirits!" It worked for a while, but I haven't found the perfect plan, so I recommend flexibility and occasionally revamping and/or ramping up the effort. Use your imagination. If dieting is needed, Weight Watchers still appears to be the best option based on results and sustainability.

In my experience, finding what works means analyzing what I like and want, then maximizing it. I like to swim, but it's boring. A mile is 64 laps in a semi-Olympic pool for Pete's sake. One way I make it less dull is to fill up my mind with a combination of meditation, prayer, planning, and reflection. I also change the stroke and use hand paddles. I hate the treadmill and the elliptical, so I distract myself with a good talk show, podcast, or some jazzy music at a decibel level that suits me. I make up contests with myself on things like increasing my heart rate. I don't like fruit, but I do like smoothies. I love vegetables, so that one's easy.

One more thing: Get to know your body and listen to it. For the first five or so decades, our bodies tick along, letting us treat them like invisible 24/7 servants. We expect them to be on tap at every moment, we pay little attention to their needs or wants, we rarely say thank you, and if they don't perform as expected, we cuss

A Palette of Strategies for Successful Aging

them out. Sadly, we can't fire them, but as they become less efficient, our tendency is to yell and tell them to shape up. We feel betrayed and dismayed by their lapses.

At the risk of sounding completely loony, I think our bodies speak to us; a body has a voice. Secretly, I think it has its own mind. It tells you when something isn't quite right, though it seldom tells you what it is or what to do unless you listen very closely, use your common sense, and respond.

A few years ago, I had a swollen, painful right knee as well as plantar fasciitis in my right foot. I also had an upcoming trip to Petra in Jordan. It's a one and a half mile desert-temperature walk into Petra unless you want to ride a donkey or a camel. So, first line of defense: I went to an orthopedist. He said I would just have to get over the plantar fasciitis and there wasn't much else to do. He also sent me for an MRI of the knee. When the x-rays came back, they showed a torn meniscus and a lot of fluid on the knee. The orthopedist said I needed surgery, but of course this wasn't possible before my trip.

I was fed up; he was obviously more interested in young men with sports injuries than old ladies. So, second line of defense: I consulted "Dr. Web"—but only reputable Internet websites like Mayo Clinic, National Institutes of Health, Harvard, and in this case, the pages of recognized orthopedic organizations. I developed a regimen of exercises for the foot and knee, faithfully applied hot and cold packs as directed, massaged my knee, and took Ibuprofen. I added one little twist: instead of cursing my leg, I spoke kindly to it. "Thank you, little leg, for so faithfully carrying me through cities, deserts, cobblestones, and ruins all over the world. I really appreciate it."

In two weeks I was fine; I walked to Petra without pain. When we were back, I went to a new orthopedist who said the liquid build-up in my knee was down by 60%.

I'm not saying this will work with cancer, but it's an example of a multi-faceted approach to your health and your body. Other ideas:

- *Use tested medical services in your community.* Find a doctor you trust who listens to you. Don't

assume he or she has all the answers, and if necessary, get a second opinion.
- *Consult reputable, reliable sources online for home and natural remedies.* Don't trust blogs or anything that's based on individual opinions.
- *Speak kindly to your body and treat it well.*
- *Get informed about your condition once it's diagnosed.* This will help you ask the right questions and interact honestly with your family and friends.
- *Read enough to know which symptoms are likely stress-related,* e.g., a lot of back pain, sciatica, migraines, etc., then actively seek to reduce the stress through rest, therapy, time with friends, meditation or counseling.
- *Don't go for outlandish cures no matter how convincing they seem.* Yes, there is a tension between "natural medicine" and the medical establishment, but some things are simply too goofy and unproven to be scientifically credible. I had a friend who did multiple coffee enemas and took 200 pig pancreas tablets a day for pancreatic cancer. She still died. Perhaps it gave her a sense of control, a more positive outlook, or eased her pain. The placebo effect is gaining credibility and shouldn't be discounted. Just remember,

one person's experiment doesn't make a "controlled study."
- *Avoid magical thinking.* There's no cure for old age. We are all terminal.

3. Strategies for mental growth

We live in the most fertile period of continuing education in human history. Learning is at our fingertips in a way it never was for our ancestors. In the eras of great libraries, only the elite had access to all that knowledge. Now, with the tap of a finger, we can access brain studies, courses from major universities in everything from art history and trigonometry to learning Chinese and anatomy. We have the Khan Academy, Coursera, Massive Open Online Courses (MOOCs), webinars, TED talks, and podcasts. We have NPR on-air and online, books on tape or Kindle, community centers, and community colleges. The opportunities are endless.

In other words, there's no excuse for not using and expanding your mind. Oh, you say, "but we lose neurons, axons, dendrites, and telomeres, etc. as we age." We forget. Our minds don't work as well. We may feel that's true, but in fact, science is making huge strides in understanding the plasticity and continual growth in brain capacity that goes on until we die. Almost without exception, the advice is "use it or lose it."

If you don't have a computer, your local library does. If you don't know how to use a computer, somebody there can help you. You can sign up for a one-day course or enlist a techie grandchild to set you up. (Be careful with the last one as most kids aren't good teachers even when they're brilliant at whizzing around the Internet.) If learning the computer is too daunting, start small with an electronic book, attend a monthly seminar on interesting topics, or simply visit the library. Do your regular crosswords or Sudoku.

Here are a few specific strategies:

- *Figure out what you want to learn.* You may have wanted to study psychology in college, but your parents said you needed to be a teacher or a nurse. Study psychology now. You may have a lifelong interest in wood-carving. Find a class. Choose your focus and go for it.

☐ *Explore resources.* Skim through the available online course providers. Go to the library. Open up the TED website and let your fingers do the walking. Talk to other people to find other options they know about.

☐ *Analyze your learning style.* Do you learn best by hearing, doing, or seeing? Do you learn best in a group or individually? Does being in a group make you anxious or awaken a healthy spirit of competition? Does the idea of a regular class time fill you with dread or confidence? How much energy are you willing to expend? Do you want a "grade" to show the world and yourself how well you've learned? The answers to these questions make a difference and will help you focus your search.

☐ *Then just do it.* Observe, judge, weigh up, decide and *act*. You can always change your mind later.

4. Strategies for economic well-being

Hopefully, you started on this one a long time ago. Regular savings do make a difference! If you're 50, you still have time to save enough for your old age, but it will require a more concerted effort than if you're 25.

This is a very complex area and I realized almost immediately upon tackling it that the variables are endless. There are *worst-case scenarios* where the strategies quickly come down to starting a garden, hoping someone else will help you out, and praying for an early death. There are *moderately-bad scenarios* where your savings are non-existent, your Social Security check is small, you're not eligible for programs like food stamps, and your kids are no help. There are *moderately-good scenarios* where your income covers the basics, but nothing more, so the end of each month is an anxious time. And there are *best-case scenarios* where you've done most things right, and between savings, pensions, Social Security, and good health, you are nicely set up for the duration.

Old age brings some tough choices. Do you stay in the family home even though it's too big and costly to maintain? Where does your health care come from? What if you're suddenly incapacitated? Do you have a designated health care proxy? Do you know your state's requirements for a living will? Do you have clear directives for your possessions and money that all your kids are aware of? Do you stay in the same town or move closer to friends or family? Where will your community come from as you age? Most of the answers to these questions have financial implications and you need to look at them head-on.

If you have difficulty making ends meet, you have only three choices. You either (1) earn more, *(2)* spend less, *or (3)* do some combination *of (1) and (2).*

Before beginning your plan for financial well-being, keep in mind the following attitudes necessary to doing a realistic assessment and process:

1. *Assume* that there's a solution to every problem.
2. *Accept* that if the problem is desperate, the solutions will probably be more drastic than you'd like—so get ready for it.
3. *Recognize* that even if your spouse handled everything financial and you don't know the first thing about it, there are resources,

both in yourself and outside, that will help you. You are strong enough to take this bull by the horns, and there are people who can teach you how to ride it.

4. *Acknowledge* that some solutions are immediate and others take time. As an old person, time is the one thing there may not be enough of, so you must be decisive.

Having the right attitudes—the ones that take you forward—will make all the difference.

The starting strategy in any of these scenarios is to evaluate your current situation and where you are on the cost-income axis, i.e. how much do you earn or save and how much do you spend? The main truth to remember is the following: *If you have difficulty making ends meet, you have* only *three choices.* You either (1) *earn more,* (2) *spend less,* or (3) *do some combination* of (1) and (2). After doing this, here are some suggestions:

☐ *Decide to be ruthlessly realistic and honest with yourself.* If you prefer not doing that, get outside help to make sure that you bite every bullet that needs to be bitten.

☐ *Do a budget.* This may seem like a no-brainer, but it's amazing how many people never do one. First determine your net monthly income (after taxes) from work, investments, and savings. Then figure out what you spend each month in the following categories: *housing* (mortgage, upkeep, repairs, renovation, yard, homeowners' insurance); *transportation* (vehicle, insurance, inspections, gas, etc.); *food* (groceries, eating out); *health care* (insurance policies, meds out of pocket, doctor visits, hospital stays); and *other* (clothing, liquor or cigarettes, donations or gifts, contributions to family members, education if you still have kids at home, pension payments if you're still working, etc.) If you want to split some of these apart and create another category, do so.

☐ *A couple of points on the budget categories above*: First, for most people, housing, transportation and food are the three largest expenses. Second, health care goes up as you age, whereas education and some of the items included in "other" tend to go down.

☐ *Determine which of the following categories your costs fall into.* (a) Some costs are *fixed*, like housing, insurance, electricity, and health care: you must pay them, they stay much the same each month, and if you don't pay, you're in big trouble. (b) Other costs are more variable, but still *mostly fixed*. For example, the price of gas may change, but the amount you use per week is much the same. The amount and cost of food may vary, but if your spouse travels or you have three hungry teenagers, you still have to feed them. (c) Finally, some costs are *not fixed*; they depend on personal choices, like new clothing, home renovation, smoking and drinking, and donations to charities or family members.

☐ *Decide how you can cut costs in each category.* This is where it gets tough. Cutting costs usually involves letting go of habits, perceptions of need, desires. And that is hard. You know the self-talk:

Yes, the house is too big and we shouldn't be going up and down steps. My spouse is unwell and I can't do the maintenance myself. How can we contemplate selling it, it's our only financial asset? Moving would be a nightmare! Where will the kids stay when they visit?

One of things that makes a move difficult is if the house represents the bulk of what is left to your heirs. You don't want to spend it on yourself, and that's understandable.

But it may be a decision that is "penny-wise and pound-foolish." If you choose to sell in order to live somewhere that reduces risk, offers community and care, it releases your family from worry and dissension. They will know and appreciate it in the long run.

Many older people put things off until their favorite options are no longer viable. Moving into a retirement center at 97 years old is much harder than it would be at 87. Waiting "until you're ready" reduces the types of places that will take you. The longer you wait, the harder it is to get past the feeling that "I've come here to die." Going in younger offers a chance to think "I'm making a new life for myself."

I realize that making a new life might not appeal to everybody. Some people passionately want life to stay the same—same house, same spouse, same routines, same security, same income. But growing older means change.

One of the lessons from Atul Gawande's book *Being Mortal*—a must-read for everyone—has been important for me. Gawande realized how deeply his father wanted to be "in control" until the end. My mother also wanted to be in control, but in a different way. She had an iron will that got her up every day at 6 a.m. to do her ablutions, dress, and put on her makeup. She insisted on that routine until three days before she died. I wanted to suggest that given her fragility and lack of balance, this wasn't wise. But it was an area of control that was so important to her, we found ways for someone to be in the vicinity while she was up. Earlier, before she opted for the retirement center, we told her she could stay in her house until she died, but given her falls and calls to 911, we were going to insist on more caregivers.

If you want independence, don't wait until you desperately need help and then demand that people leave you alone and let you decide.

Her choice wasn't unlimited, but it was a real choice: (a) more strangers taking care of her at home, or (b) friends who checked on her at the retirement home. In the end, she made the right choice, and she was able to die in her "home" with neighbors stopping by and wishing her well.

Change is the name of the game. If *you* don't make the changes, someone else will. Financial flexibility gives you more choice in designing the future you want, but it still can be done on a limited budget—just not with a limited mind.

5. Strategies for spiritual deepening

This is a tricky one. Frankly, I wonder how anyone grows old well without having a foundational belief that there's more to life than what we can see. Spirituality is big.

I'm using "spiritual" in the broadest possible sense. For some, it is a simple recognition that we all have wisdom, a voice, a deep Self that is smarter than we are, "a mystery that looms within and arches beyond the limits of my being."[*] For others it is more orthodox, a traditional belief embodied in an institutional religion, whether Christianity, Islam, Buddhism, Judaism, or another enduring faith. The spectrum between those two poles is vast and varied, but one common thread is an acknowledgement of

---

[*] F. Forrester Church, *Everyday Miracles: Stories from Life*

the "ineffable" or unexplainable mystery in life and the need for a personal belief system that gives voice to that experience.

I don't care what you call it. I don't care about the doctrines or theological frameworks that accompany it. I do care that your beliefs visibly enhance your life and can be seen in your actions and attitudes. When I see someone who embodies love, forgiveness, and inclusiveness, when he or she clearly lives what they say they believe, I know that person is aging well. Some people who use religious language constantly also lie or whine or ignore others' suffering. Likewise there are so-called "heathens" who evidence all the characteristics of goodness. I think of a friend who was quite anti-religious, but began each day with a period for reflecting on how she would be of service during the day and how she could have a positive effect in each person's life. Her attention encompassed everyone from close friends to anonymous bus drivers.

Why include "spiritual deepening" in a discussion of strategies for aging well? It's a way to enlarge our life while aging is shrinking our world.

Our physical world shrinks because we have less ability or energy to navigate it. Our mental world may shrink with more limited opportunities for dialogue, debate, and engagement with new ideas; we tend to surround ourselves with others who think like we do. Our emotional world shrinks because we become more interested in maintaining our personal sphere of control than in reaching out and supporting others, we struggle with sadness and depression, or we become fearful. We are susceptible to self-absorption.

Life is further reduced when we passively allow old age to sweep us along rather than daring to confront it and use it to our advantage. The image of the "wise elder" still lingers, but what do we mean? Perhaps it describes a person who has taken all of his or her experience, plumbed its meaning, and is willing to share it. It is a person of "heft"and substance, humility, depth, and lightness of spirit. It is a person who cares for others even as others care for them.

What are the advantages of aging vis-à-vis spiritual deepening? First, we have time to explore our own inner worlds. We no longer strive for breadth, always seeking new experiences; rather, we have both the freedom and the opportunity to go for depth in our living. Not all old people are wise, but those who are serve as examples and mentors to everyone who knows them. Elders become wise when they know themselves, have a positive story that weaves together the dark and light of their lives, share insights from both their knowledge and their experience, acknowledge that they don't have all the answers, and are still learning. Everyone wants to be considered wise, especially if we're no longer beautiful, handsome, productive, or even mobile.

A second advantage is that the world's spiritual traditions include universal themes like love, service, compassion, self-knowledge, acceptance, and mystery. The truths these themes convey serve us well at a time when so much is happening that feels hard, unfair, and inexplicable. A healthy spiritual foundation that includes these principles takes us out of ourselves, our little lives, and our solitude. A perspective that life is meaningful is desperately needed as we age.

Without an evolving framework for living deeper than what we see, it's easy to become bitter. Many do, and we would not call them "wise."

Here are some strategies for this great exploration:

- ☐ *Define what you mean by "spirit" or the "spiritual dimension."* Why explore it? What role can it play for you as you age? What do you want as your personal *take-away* or results from this area of life? In other words, create a role and a reason for why working on *being* is worth the effort.

- ☐ *Evaluate your current practices for tapping into the spiritual dimension.* A *practice* is a regularly scheduled activity for getting in touch with your inner life. There's value in spontaneous or serendipitous events that wake us up, but don't confuse them with practices. Common practices include solitary reflection at the beginning or end of the day; prayer, meditation, contemplation, either alone or combined with exercise; and intentional exercise like walking, running, swimming, yoga, Qigong, etc. Other options are writing in a journal, using art and music to inspire you and "stop the world," reading literature or a religious text, writing poetry, talking to a close friend or counselor. Which of these do you do? Which are satisfying? Which aren't? What are some new avenues you can explore? The practices you choose form an important piece of the personal lattice that I introduced at the beginning of this chapter.

☐ *Here's one exercise that's helped me.* I said earlier that I simultaneously swim and meditate. One of my meditations involves choosing three alliterative qualities I want to emphasize. To date, I've focused on *patience-presence-playfulness, discipline-discernment-delight, exploration-expressiveness-enthusiasm, awareness-affirmation-appreciation*, and more, but you get the idea. I do each set for a year when I swim. I apply each quality to the day ahead. I think about where I'm struggling and how I can more effectively embody each. I have felt twinges of "improvement" in the sense that having these categories makes me more conscious of my actions, both when I fall short and when I do okay.

☐ *Create time and space for personal sharing.* My husband and I read a short poem or passage from a book at breakfast, then talk. One of our favorite sources is Rachel Naomi Remen's *My Grandfather's Blessings*. Another is Garrison Keillor's *The Writer's Almanac*.

Yet another is poems by Mary Oliver or Billy Collins. We've recently discovered *The Book of Joy*, conversations between Desmond Tutu and the Dalai Lama. The conversation partner you choose needs to be someone with whom you feel comfortable opening up deeper topics. Common ways to do this are regular get-togethers with close friends, book clubs, discussion groups with defined themes, intentional tours (e.g., tours that focus on art, music, culture, or world religions). The point here is to create settings in which you can give voice to personal fears, concerns, insights, or revelations.

☐ *Write down your dreams.* It may seem odd to put this as a strategy, but in fact, dreams can make us aware of problems, possibilities, or ideas that we may be ignoring in our waking life. If you have an anxiety dream every other night, it's worth examining why this might be. If you have a particularly vivid dream that you sense has a message, explore it. There are many approaches to dream analysis, but one I like is to think of each character as an aspect of yourself, then to talk with each one, asking why they showed up or what they're trying to say. This can be both fun and full of insight into your inner life.

☐ *Explore other belief systems.* There are good readings on world religions like those of Huston Smith. There are individual books like *The Fragrance of Faith* by Jamal Rahman (Islam) or *Awakening the Buddha Within* by Lama Surya Das (Buddhism). There are books like *The Heart of Christianity* by Marcus Borg. There are many other authors who challenge our notions of religion, faith, ethics, and morality. Practice an open mind. Aging can cause us to shut down any perspectives outside what we've honed over our many years. Allowing fresh air into our interior landscape can only be helpful.

6. Strategies for creating your legacy

I can't over-emphasize the mandate to *take responsibility while you can.* If you want independence, don't wait until you desperately need help and then demand that people leave you alone and let you decide. If you want a say in your care, design your old age in advance. *Above all, don't make your children or anyone you love do it for you.* Frankly, that's a crappy legacy. How many times have you heard:

Why should we clear out the books or clean the basement? Our kids can do it when we die! Or, no, I don't have a will; lawyers are too expensive and the kids know what we want.

If I ask, "Are you going to die?" you will say "Of course." Yet if I ask you to describe your plan for old age—with questions like do you have a DNR (Do Not Resuscitate Order)? A will? Who gets the jewelry? Where will you live? What will you do if your spouse dies first? What if you break your hip? or What's your rehab center of choice?—many of you could only stammer. But if something unforeseen happens, you are likely to fight like hell against someone else making the decisions. Frankly, you've left them no choice.

I remember a conversation with my husband and brother-in-law many years ago. We were talking about legacy and the two guys wanted to have a positive impact through their contributions to Central America or a university. Ideally they would leave something that had their names on it. My sister-in-law and I wanted our kids, family, and friends to love us and remember us as fun to be with.

I mention this because there are different ways to define "legacy." We all leave one. It can be anything from money to a set of values to creating a loving home to nothing but bad memories. A legacy is what lives past our dying, what resides in lives we touched for a time after we go. Consider that few people are famous a century after their deaths, and "residue" doesn't sound very exciting. But in fact, you are going to leave something. Why not decide now what it is and begin to shape it?

Usually, when people talk about legacy, they are thinking about financial inheritance, memorabilia, jewels, a business, foundation, or organization they have built. Yes, these are tangible bequests, the external legacies everyone can see. They are important, but there are intangible bequests like values, memories, sayings, and attitudes that are at least, if not more, important. Who do people say you were? Why were you someone to emulate, or not? What did they learn from you? The answers to these questions are drawn both from your own self-knowledge and from asking others, hoping for an honest response.

A few suggestions for thinking about your legacy:

☐ *Decide what you want people to remember about you.* What values, qualities, achievements, attitudes, and wisdom do you hope they take from sharing their lives with you? What gifts do you want to give—letters, jewelry, and family heirlooms or keepsakes, art, and crafts? Are there specific people who want specific things? Clearly designate any bequests that are meaningful to you or responsive to others' wishes.

In your list of legacies, include things like *reconciliation, peace, no regrets,* and the like. Think about how to make this happen. One family I know is made up of four children (in their 50s and 60s) and one demented father who is living in the family home, an old, run-down house. He misspent a large amount of money, so has nothing to leave as an inheritance. Everyone is angry about that, but it's too late to recoup. There is no consensus among the kids as to his future. One insists that he shouldn't be moved, yet resents the time she spends caretaking and managing caretakers. One insists a move to a facility is the only logical response. Two are betwixt and between, depending on which sibling they're with. This family is in trouble, and it's hard to believe their father's "legacy" will be anything other than bitter regret and ongoing anger. No one wants to leave a legacy like that.

☐ *Think about* how *you die.* Yes, I know most people hope they drop dead or die in their sleep, but we may not get our wish. It is possible, however, to decide how you want to die—not the cause or the moment or the specifics of it—but the attitudes with which you receive death. The Buddhists recommend daily contemplation on your dying and they cite individuals who have demonstrated quiet acceptance of the inevitable and an ability to reach out with love until the moment they lose consciousness. If a child, grandchild, or good friend is sitting by your bed, what do you want them to remember about your final moments? The odd thing about this exercise is the way it throws you back into *life* and raises the question of how you want to live knowing your zone of control may be tiny or non-existent at the end.

☐ *What conversations do you need to have with your spouse, children, or friends?* Are there conflicts that need to be resolved? Is everyone clear about your wishes? One of the saddest things is watching a family fall apart upon the death of the person who was the glue. When there are fights over money or a favorite chest of drawers or the china, hostilities are put into place that can last until everyone dies and even into the next generation. You can make that an unlikely scenario by ensuring resolution and clarity now. The best way to do this is to *write it down*. That said, you can't entirely eliminate the chance of unresolved conflict. Every conflict has two sides and if one side is willing to forgive and move on, and one is intransigent to the end, reconciliation is nigh unto impossible.

What do you do then? My only suggestion is to write a letter, leave a gift, or do something that unmistakably signals forgiveness. One example of this was a friend who suffered three strokes in quick succession, but who stayed alive (and I think aware, in spite of being unresponsive) until her two estranged children arrived. Even though nothing was said, there was closure and healing that wouldn't have been there without that final visit. She died a half hour after they left the hospital.

☐ *Do you have any special requests?* Let people know what they are. One friend asked that her favorite hymns be played or sung by anyone who was with her as she died. Another friend was accompanied by her family reading messages, poems, meaningful quotations sent by people from all over the world as well as by a 24-hour prayer cycle of volunteers. I was struck by both the symbolic and practical aspects of these actions, both of which added rich significance and meaning to the event, especially for the living.

☐ *How will you communicate love and forgiveness to each person who needs to hear that from you?* I had two friends—a man and a woman—who wrote beautiful letters toward the end of their lives. One died of lung cancer, the other of pancreatic cancer. Both had chosen to send out a group letter that expressed their gratitude for friendships, support given in each phase of their lives as well as their deep recognition and acceptance of the inevitability of their passing. It was profoundly moving in both instances. Although I was much closer to the woman and hardly knew the man, both of their letters gave me pause and pushed me to think about my own final message.

These examples hint at the deeper nature of legacy, namely what we take away as conscious remembrances of a friend or loved one. Knowing and accepting our deaths gives us an opportunity to think about a legacy that will continue after we're gone.

CHAPTER 5

When is it Time To Create a New Future?

How do you know it's time to make changes? The day will come, when if you haven't decided, someone else will. Even if you don't live into your 90s, when you begin to fall regularly or you are found wandering in a mall or your house begins to reek of neglect, someone will be there to put the issue of increased support right in the middle of the table. That's if you're blessed with someone who cares enough to do so.

There's no "one-size-fits-all" description of that day, but here are a few things to keep in mind:

1. *The earlier you start imagining your future as an old person*, the less shocking it will be when you realize that everyone else sees you that way. I'm still amazed when people offer me their seats or take my arm to go down steps. *Do I look that old?* I say to myself. The answer is *yes*. If you've done the homework of designing your future, you'll respond more positively when friends and family intervene to ensure your well-being. One day my husband Harry pointed out my tendency to refuse friends' attempts to help me with curbs and steps, which are dangerous because I'm going blind. He said I needed to respond with a sincere "Thank you, I think I can manage it" or "Thank you, I'll take you up on the offer." I was a tiny bit offended, but he was so right. I felt better and so did my friends.

2. *Every person is unique in his or her readiness to accept additional help or to move to a community*, whether continuing care, assisted living, nursing home, or whatever, but if we live long enough, we will reach the time when we need more care. There's no hard and fast formula for making decisions about future living arrangements. A strong indicator that a decision is imminent is when you're spending too much time trying

to fool everyone into believing you're fine. Wake up when that happens. In my mother's case, she fell more than she told us; she could see far less than we imagined. It was only when she moved into the retirement home that we realized how close to blind she was. She insisted on eating out, then said she didn't like the food. Whether she was scared to swallow or couldn't see the plate or had lost her taste, I don't know. I only know that keeping up a front went on too long, and we allowed her to do it because we're conflict averse.

3. *There are often social or cultural factors to be taken into account.* As long as a couple is a couple, they often want to stay together until the end, even if one is much needier than the other. The healthier one may feel that he or she can't "give up" because of a potentially harsh judgment by other people. Death may cause the remaining spouse either to dig in his or her heels against change or to make impulsive decisions (like marrying too quickly), or it may serve to push them to new options.

Outside North America, families tend to stay closer geographically. The kids live in the same city and are therefore more available. The norm in many cultures is that parents move in with their children when the time comes. The phenomenon of "over-50 communities" or even nursing homes is still embryonic and stigmatized. Even if a parent has lived in the US for many years, he or she may harbor the same expectations. If one sibling has remained in the home country while others have relocated, they may also have difficulty accepting the idea of a community care facility. We need to be aware of the social or cultural narratives behind peoples' expectations for care, autonomy, and community in old age.

4. *A compelling, logical argument can be made for virtually every scenario.* That's to say that every option has plusses and minuses. It's likely that each affected person—child, spouse, or sibling—has an "airtight rationale" for his or her recommended course of action. Intransigence, however, can lead to extreme conflict in the family. Every option—staying at home, living with the kids, moving into a retirement community, hiring additional care—has advantages and disadvantages, costs and benefits. So don't expect the "what next?" discussion to be easy. Be on the lookout for unrealistic hopes, the most common of which is "Maybe he or she will get better...." At a certain age, we don't get better.

When Is It Time To Create a New Future?

When the main caregivers disagree over what should happen, it may be necessary to bring in a third party. This mediator can be a minister, hospice worker, doctor—any outsider whose role is to help people listen to each other, empathize, confront reality, determine feasible scenarios, and reach a consensus.

My experience with Mother seems typical of many in the US. My brother and I first invited Mom to move near one of us. He lives a couple of hours away and I live overseas; like many families, we're scattered. Either way, she couldn't imagine leaving the town she had lived in since birth.

Then we encouraged her to stop driving when she turned 90. I even called the Texas Department of Public Safety to see if they would fail her. They laughed. I asked my brother if he knew anyone who would steal the car. He didn't. So she renewed her license, which was good to age 97. She finally stopped driving after coming to an intersection and finding herself unable to tell whether the light was red or green.

She was falling more, and we suggested home care, knowing how desperately she didn't want to move to a retirement place. Her response was, "I can't live in a *box*." She rejected the idea of even minimal home help. "What will I do with all those *strangers* in the house?" When we discovered a small but significant heart irregularity after a late-night 911 call and trip to the hospital, we got a little tougher. Maintaining the status quo was no longer an option. We gave her two choices: She could either have more regular care in her home or she could move to the local retirement center where a friend lived. She went for a visit to the center and after some deliberation, agreed to move in. But then she got cold feet. "The room is too small and I'm claustrophobic. I can't be on the second floor. I have to ride the elevator and I'm claustrophobic." After weeks of wrangling, my brother put his foot down and she moved. After six months of griping, she began to appreciate the people and the place.

From this daughter's point of view, this was a truly difficult period. You want to care for this person who's cared for you. You want their end days to be fulfilling and as pleasant as possible. You want them to be safe. If you're far away, you want to be assured someone is watching over them. And many times, they resent your interference, fighting you at every step, demanding independence when it's no longer warranted by facts. Mother would say, "I know you and your brother are worried," but I could tell our feelings didn't really matter in her battle to maintain the status quo.

> *...each crisis provokes a re-thinking, a conscious decision to look at options for where and how you will live. Any one of them could lead to a new decision.*

As the child, you're beset by behaviors and expectations you've had since you were a kid. Your parents have always been your *parents*. They may need your help, but they're loath to let you play the parent role. You're afraid of offending them, causing a breach that doesn't heal before the end, and this stalemate leaves you wondering which way to go.

All of these factors combine to make decision-making a muddy and confusing process. I can't tell you how many people I've met who are facing this situation. In one family, the parents owned their home and seemed well-fixed financially. Then a conversation between siblings revealed that the parents had asked one brother for $40,000, which he willingly gave, but which hadn't been mentioned since. The only reason the problem came to light was because then his sister was asked for $20,000. It was so unusual, she mentioned it to her brother and then asked her folks why they needed the money. She ran into a wall of silence. Since the children were well-off professionals, the discovery that their parents were in financial trouble provoked an immediate emotional response and desire to help. The parents still refused to say what the problem was, leaving the four brothers and sisters with the dreadful dilemma of being "the bad guys" for pushing for an answer. As I write, the siblings still aren't clear about what's happening and are struggling with guilt, frustration, confusion, and anger.

When Is It Time To Create a New Future?

If my brother and I hadn't been on the same page, which we were, thanks to Mom's initiative, it would have been a thousand times worse. My advice: Listen to your parents—more than I did. Affirm the authenticity of their fears and their profound belief that they can do this on their own, but ask questions that might guide them to an understanding of this phase and its limits like: What is it costing—emotionally, physically, financially—to care for the house and/or each other? Ask if they have anything in writing that ensures that those left behind know unequivocally what they want done. Help everyone involved discern the most viable options, which might not be the ones they want, but are the only realistic ones. Don't get mad at them if you can help it, which I couldn't from time to time. Practice compassionate toughness as much as possible. Bite the bullet when it comes to being the bad guy (or gal), and have someplace where you can cry and holler and throw pillows, because it's sad and frustrating.

Parents, do you really want to do this to your kids?

Deciding to change a life pattern of many years is wrenching. Some people look the challenge in the face and just do it. I was surprised to discover a woman about my age living in Mom's retirement center, so I made a point to find out her story. She was a single career woman with no children, who had discovered that she had Parkinson's Disease. She simply felt that she needed to begin a new life in a close-knit community with a smaller space, less maintenance, and a good balance of personal and group time. Another woman moved after losing her home when a fertilizer plant exploded and her husband to a heart attack a week later. She courageously made a move that offered her a different kind of support. Each person had a unique story. There is no template for making the change, though I think there are indicators about the right time to decide. Significantly, the happiest people in Mother's place were those who had deliberately chosen to live there versus being forced in by family or friends.

I have several suggestions:

When Is It Time To Create a New Future?

- If you're 70 or older, establish criteria for knowing when it's time to make a major change like moving into a smaller place, going into a planned community, or hiring help. The age limit for me is 75 and 80 for my husband. The age is arbitrary, but it gives us an objective deadline. Our criteria include:
  - when our current community is diminishing and our isolation is increasing
  - when we're fully retired
  - when one of us can no longer drive
  - when we can no longer adequately care for the other's needs
  - when memory lapses, like leaving the broiler on or getting lost, have potentially disastrous consequences
  - when there's a major crisis like a broken hip, car accident, or illness
  - when routine maintenance, like changing the light bulbs, becomes onerous
  - when one of us dies

Obviously, you don't wait for all these things to happen. Rather, each crisis provokes a re-thinking, a conscious decision to look at options for where and how you will live. Any one of them could lead to a new decision.

In our case, we want to move to a community while we are both lucid and autonomous, while we can still enjoy life outside four walls, while we have the energy to engage in the activities, e.g., college courses, art classes, volunteerism, and trips that many places offer. We want to establish the community we will die in and to feel we are contributors, not only to it, but to the larger world. We want to be in a place where our kids can visit and where they feel we are looked after.

- Be ready to explain your decision to people who care about you. It's no one's life but yours and it's extremely important to take full responsibility for your choices. Mother often said to me, "You know, I could die in this house or fall and be here three days before anyone would notice." I recognized her fear because I was also afraid and eventually said to her, "That's the decision you're making by opting to live alone. If it's not the outcome you want, you need to get some systems in place for you to get help." She didn't like that much, but it was the truth. Actually, I established the system and called her daily for years after that conversation. I'm not sure it assuaged her fear as much as it assuaged mine.

- If you really love your children, friends or relatives, you will *not* force them to make this decision for you. Don't make them choose where and how you will die. The very least you can do is give them your criteria and some solid direction. Don't hogtie them, but also don't leave loose ends. Otherwise, there will be rifts, hurt, and anger, and what a lousy way for things to end. Each of the people who care about you will have a good reason for his or her scenario of what should happen, and somebody has to win. Save them from fighting a war to see who that will be.

CHAPTER 6

Final Thoughts

The importance of resilience

An underlying motif in everything I've written is *resilience*. Merriam-Webster's definition is twofold:

(a) the ability to become strong, healthy, or successful again after something bad happens

(b) the ability of something to return to its original shape after it has been pulled, stretched, pressed, bent, etc.

Taking definition (a), my assumption is that you, dear reader, are strong enough to rebound after something bad happens. Many people think that growing old and dying is a really "bad" something. I don't agree, but I will concede that aging is filled with a bunch of less-than-wonderful moments and huge challenges. No one knows exactly where resilience comes from, but it's an equal-opportunity quality. It shows up in young and old, the educated and uneducated, the well-off and the dirt-poor, the healthy and the sick, the happy and the sad, those who have had halcyon lives and those for whom life has been a ceaseless battle.

Is it simply the "luck of the birth lottery" or can it be developed? Obviously, some factors retard resilience: genetic propensities to clinical depression or mental illness, or long-term exposure to a negative environment. But a remarkable range of people have within themselves, and maybe within their cells, an ability to become strong, healthy, and successful even after tragedies. I believe resilience is learnable.

As for definition (b), more commonly applied to scientific phenomena or rubber bands, I would suggest that for most of us, our "original shape" is one of wholeness, courage, health,

Final Thoughts

and strength, and that in spite of the fact that life pulls, stretches, presses, and bends us, we don't completely lose the ability to be the self we most want to be. This is not easy. In fact, it's really, really hard.

It is, however, worth the effort to cultivate resilience. It may come naturally or it may seem to be absent, but the truth is that either way, we can create attitudes and take actions that strengthen the ability to rebound, and to use every hurdle life gives us to build mental and spiritual muscle.

A Message to the Sandwich Generation

I'm probably talking to folks of a certain age who are either aging artfully or at least thinking about how to do so. I hope there are a few readers from the "What a morbid subject!" group. I also hope there are some younger ones.

I'm writing for many reasons, but among them is my empathy with "The Sandwich Generation"—those of us caught between struggling kids and struggling parents. This time can begin as early as age forty, so it isn't only people with 90-year-old parents. It's a varied demographic, but most agree that it's not an easy or happy time.

I was fortunate to have a mother who recognized me until 48 hours before she died. She had given my brother and me the tools we needed to sail the stormy waters of dying and death. She was in a loving, clean, safe environment with people she had come to know, and we were able to afford the necessary care, using both her resources and ours. So many things came together. Her granddaughters rallied around. Her neighbors and the employees of the retirement home, from the kitchen staff to the director, were generous and kind. I never felt abandoned, as many people do.

That's not to say, however, that I didn't feel alone. Watching someone die is very hard. Each person's death leaves a void, sometimes blessedly free of regrets, and other times, darkened by unspoken words, resentments, recriminations, shame, and rage. I was blessed with a void that was largely free of those things, but like any death, it marked the end of new possibilities for reconciliation. My mother was *my* mother, and only secondarily my brother's mother or her granddaughters' grandmother or Peggy's friend. You're alone with your loss, whatever that may be.

How can they cope with the death of the relationship when the person is still alive? It is a hellish experience, but...you don't need to go through it alone.

I was also fortunate that Mother was "with the program" mentally in addition to being in an optimal care situation. Too many of my generation can't say the same. They have parents who don't recognize them, don't remember a visit from yesterday, scream at them, or have memories that aren't real. Their parents may hurt or exclude them, or behave in ways that are alien and disturbing. How can they cope with the death of the relationship when the person is still alive? It is a hellish experience, but if this is your situation, you don't need to go through it alone. Seek advice from those who work hand-in-hand with dementia or Alzheimer's to bring your expectations into line with the reality. Seek an advisor. Create a new narrative, as well as a schedule that offers a respite from the sad frustration of caring for those in this situation.

Losing a spouse
The death of a husband or wife is a very specific loss. If your marriage was loving and satisfying, the void is complete and shocking. One widow told me she never fully realized all the things her husband did, from finances and trip planning to romantic gestures. On the other hand, if the marriage was less than wonderful, you may be left with regrets or resentment.

There are many responses. Several male friends' wives died before them. One spent several months helping his adult children come to terms with the loss of their mother. Then he began traveling, first a week at a time, then longer; first alone, then with a family friend, a good friend of his late wife who may now be more than "just a friend." Another widower quickly replaced his wife of forty years with a woman his kids' age who has yet to fit into her husband's circle of 70-plus cronies. Another friend has struggled with clinical depression in the form of lethargy, hopelessness, and distractedness. Her son thinks she may be getting dementia, but I suspect she's just stuck in grief and sees no way out.

I am more conscious of decisions about trips we take, events we attend, and people we see.

Men and women sometimes handle the death of a spouse differently, but there are common denominators. Whether their loved one suffered through a long, painful bout of cancer or dropped dead in an instant, they usually have the experience Joan Didion beautifully describes in *The Year of Magical Thinking*, written after the sudden loss of her husband and subsequent loss of her only daughter. The time after is full of shock and emptiness. It slowly dawns that the other is truly dead. Each day is filled with fear, sadness, and a vacuum of meaning and hope. Many people comment on the banality of sympathy and the absence of friends who don't know what to say. They struggle to redefine their lives for this new era even as they yearn to perpetuate the one just ended.

As difficult as it is, we *have* to recognize that one of us will go first, though I'm still hoping for a plane crash with both Harry and me on board. Every now and then, I force myself to think of life without him. I encourage him to do the same. Why? First, because this sad meditation helps me to appreciate him in a fresh way, to make the most of our life together, and to give thanks for the laughter, closeness and delight in the relationship. It also makes me aware of what he does that I either can't or don't want to do, and that forces me to learn certain things I'd just as soon not learn. I am more conscious of decisions about trips we take, events we attend, and people we see. I now evaluate their value and importance, so am less likely to stumble mindlessly through mere busy-ness. It also prompts me to make sure that my will and trust are in shape, my bequests are clear, and I've left the necessary information on bank accounts, credit cards, insurance policies, etc.

Final Thoughts

These actions are one way of loving those who will be left, loving the man I love, and loving even myself.

Finding our way home

Maybe you've heard the saying, "If you haven't been to Peoria, you haven't been to Peoria." There are many experiences we simply haven't had, yet we act like we understand them.

I haven't been to the Peoria of widowhood. Neither am I African-American, so I've never been stopped by the police for no reason. I haven't reached 90 years old, so I don't know how that feels. Some people act like they've been to Peoria when they haven't. Folks with no kids have great advice for parents. Twenty-year-olds have beautiful ideas for the elderly. Privileged people have a plan for under-privileged people. Acting like "we've been there" is the way of the world.

The fact that I am an observer rather than a full participant in certain experiences means the most I can do is sympathize and imagine my reactions. I can try to put myself in another's place. I can acknowledge the vast plain of what I don't know and the even vaster plain of what I don't know that I don't know.

Once acknowledged, I must seek understanding by talking with those who are living an experience, with the very old, those of another race, creed, gender, those who are poor or marginalized, people in a different political party or culture. That is the path of balance. In other words, I have to listen and learn. Observe. Ask questions. If dealing with a mother or father who is refusing to consider a retirement home, first listen. Ask what their concerns and fears are. Ask about the implications for the future. Ask many more questions, and listen to the answers. Parents may be old, but they're not stupid, so treat them like they know something. Challenge them. Work toward shared solutions.

If your best friend is widowed, listen to the litanies of grief. When you don't understand, ask her to talk further. I remember after my dad died, Mother suddenly wanted to install an electric garage door. I asked why she'd want one after 45 years in the house without it. She

Final Thoughts

said, "There might be a burglar waiting for me." I said, "There hasn't been a burglar for 45 years." She said, "Well, if there had been, your daddy would have protected me." I said, "But he would have lost." Then she said, "Yes, but he would have died trying." So we installed an electric door.

Listen lovingly, observe, ask questions, challenge, but let go of your agendas.

This was only the first example of my mother's fear level shooting through the roof and I've observed this in others. A self-reliant person suddenly seems uncertain about the simplest things or a recently bereaved friend immediately sets up a Match.com account. My advice for responding to a grieving parent, child, or friend: Suspend judgment, especially if it hasn't happened to you. Listen lovingly, observe, ask questions, challenge, but let go of your agendas.

Trust the currents in the sea of life. We all make it home eventually.

Epilogue

I had a dream in which a man was telling me a story. He said that as a young boy, his mother told him that when he was feeling sad, hurt, or angry, he should go for a walk, pick up a leaf, and sit with it until he could see the beauty and miracle of it. Then he should put the leaf in a sack and when the sack was full, return the leaves to the forest.

It was a gently symbolic and instructive dream. Take something ordinary, something we don't notice from day to day, and look at it until its mystery and wonder become apparent. As I contemplated the dream, I saw my own life: how seldom I sit with the ordinary things and allow them time to unfold, how I walk past the daily miracles without a second thought, how I let busy-ness sap my time and energy.

In a sense, I'm offering this small book to encourage others to look at the ordinary things of their lives long enough to see through to the possibility in them. Growing old is ordinary. Taking care of aging parents is ordinary. Even death is ordinary.

But too often, we let anxiety or ego or fear outrun the ability to take these universal experiences and explore them until we figure out their meaning for us.

And so I look at the "leaves" that are my hands. I see the visible veins, the brown spots, the swollen joints and stubby fingernails. They are no longer the smooth, soft, strong attachments they once were. But these hands caressed beloved faces, brought coffee to breakfast tables, wrote ideas on whiteboards, held babies, opened jars, and wiped away tears. They still do most of those things and more. They have a history that is rich and meaningful. They have a history no one else will ever know. They are ordinary, yet

Epilogue

symbolic of grasping and letting go, holding and discarding, loving and hating. I have the whole world in my hands. And so do you.

RECOMMENDED READING

These are books that have contributed to my personal narratives about aging and dying. Some of them are well-written, others not so much; some have only one or two excellent images, others are worthwhile cover-to-cover. All are available as electronic books. Note especially Atul Gawande's *Being Mortal: Medicine and What Matters in the End*. It is a must read. The books are listed in alphabetical order by the last name of the principal author.

Maggie Callanan and Patricia Kelley (2012). *Final Gifts: Understanding the Special Awareness, Needs, and Communications of the Dying*

Joan Chittister (2010), *The Gift of Years: Growing Older Gracefully*

Atul Gawande (2017). *Being Mortal: Medicine and What Matters in the End*

Gail Godwin (2003). *Evenings at Five*

Joan Halifax (2009). *Being with Dying: Cultivating Compassion and Fearlessness in the Presence of Death*

Chip Heath and Dan Heath (2010). *Switch: How to Change Things When Change is Hard*

Sherwin B. Nuland (1995). *How We Die: Reflections of Life's Final Chapter*

Karl Pillemer, PhD (2012). *30 Lessons for Living: Tried and True Advice from the Wisest Americans*

Rachel Naomi Remen (2001). *My Grandfather's Blessings: Stories of Strength, Refuge and Belonging*

Richard Rohr (2011). *Falling Upward: A Spirituality for the Two Halves of Life*

Sheryl Sandberg and Adam Grant (2017). *Option B: Facing Adversity, Building Resilience, and Finding Joy*

Bryan Stevenson (2015). *Just Mercy: A Story of Justice and Redemption*

Made in the USA
Columbia, SC
08 October 2018